THE JACKSONVILLE JAGUARS

BY JOANNE MATTERN

EPIC

BELLWETHER MEDIA ★ MINNEAPOLIS, MN

EPIC BOOKS are no ordinary books. They burst with intense action, high-speed heroics, and shadows of the unknown. Are you ready for an Epic adventure?

This book is intended for educational use. Organization and franchise logos are trademarks of the National Football League (NFL). This is not an official book of the NFL. It is not approved by or connected with the NFL.

This edition first published in 2024 by Bellwether Media, Inc.

No part of this publication may be reproduced in whole or in part without written permission of the publisher. For information regarding permission, write to Bellwether Media, Inc., Attention: Permissions Department, 6012 Blue Circle Drive, Minnetonka, MN 55343.

Library of Congress Cataloging-in-Publication Data

Names: Mattern, Joanne, 1963- author.
Title: The Jacksonville Jaguars / by Joanne Mattern.
Description: Minneapolis, MN : Bellwether Media, 2024. | Series: Epic. NFL team profiles | Includes bibliographical references and index. | Audience: Ages 7-12 | Audience: Grades 2-3 | Summary: "Engaging images accompany information about the Jacksonville Jaguars. The combination of high-interest subject matter and light text is intended for students in grades 2 through 7"-- Provided by publisher.
Identifiers: LCCN 2023021974 (print) | LCCN 2023021975 (ebook) | ISBN 9798886874808 (library binding) | ISBN 9798886876680 (ebook)
Subjects: LCSH: Jacksonville Jaguars (Football team)--History--Juvenile literature.
Classification: LCC GV956.J33 M37 2024 (print) | LCC GV956.J33 (ebook) | DDC 796.332/6409759/12--dc23/eng/20230517
LC record available at https://lccn.loc.gov/2023021974
LC ebook record available at https://lccn.loc.gov/2023021975

Text copyright © 2024 by Bellwether Media, Inc. EPIC and associated logos are trademarks and/or registered trademarks of Bellwether Media, Inc.

Editor: Betsy Rathburn   Designer: Jeffrey Kollock

Printed in the United States of America, North Mankato, MN.

TABLE OF CONTENTS

WHAT A RUN!	4
THE HISTORY OF THE JAGUARS	6
THE JAGUARS TODAY	14
GAME DAY!	16
JACKSONVILLE JAGUARS FACTS	20
GLOSSARY	22
TO LEARN MORE	23
INDEX	24

WHAT A RUN!

The Jaguars face the Dolphins in a 2000 **playoff** game. **Running back** Fred Taylor gets the ball.

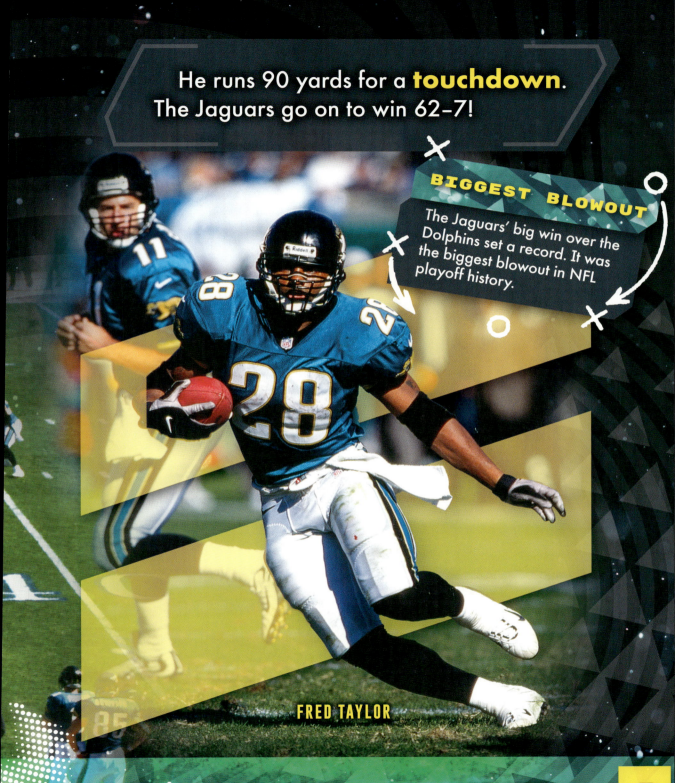

He runs 90 yards for a **touchdown**. The Jaguars go on to win 62–7!

BIGGEST BLOWOUT

The Jaguars' big win over the Dolphins set a record. It was the biggest blowout in NFL playoff history.

FRED TAYLOR

THE HISTORY OF THE JAGUARS

In 1995, the National Football League (NFL) added two new teams. One of them was the Jacksonville Jaguars.

Tackle Tony Boselli was the first player on the team. Many people think he is one of their best-ever players.

1995 JAGUARS

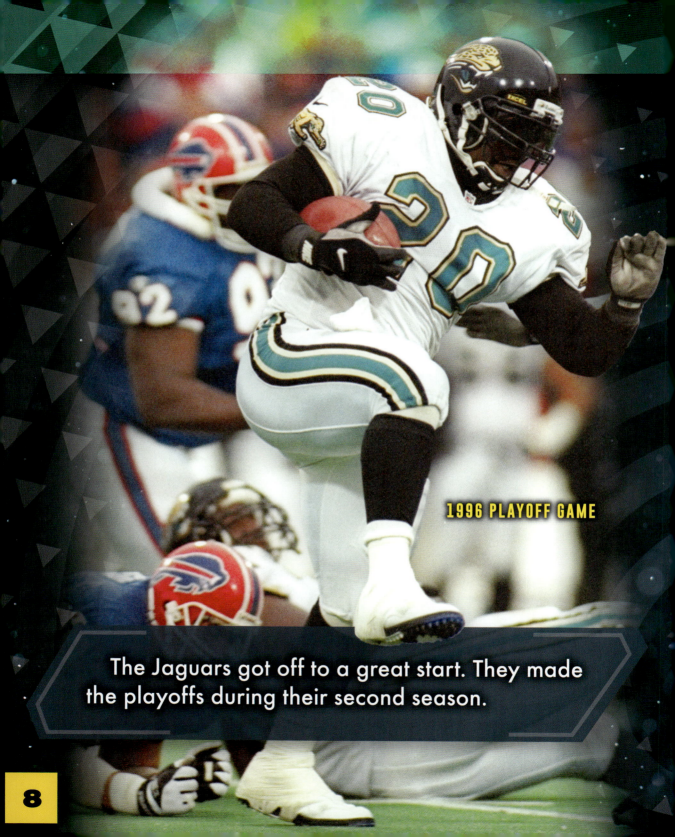

1996 PLAYOFF GAME

The Jaguars got off to a great start. They made the playoffs during their second season.

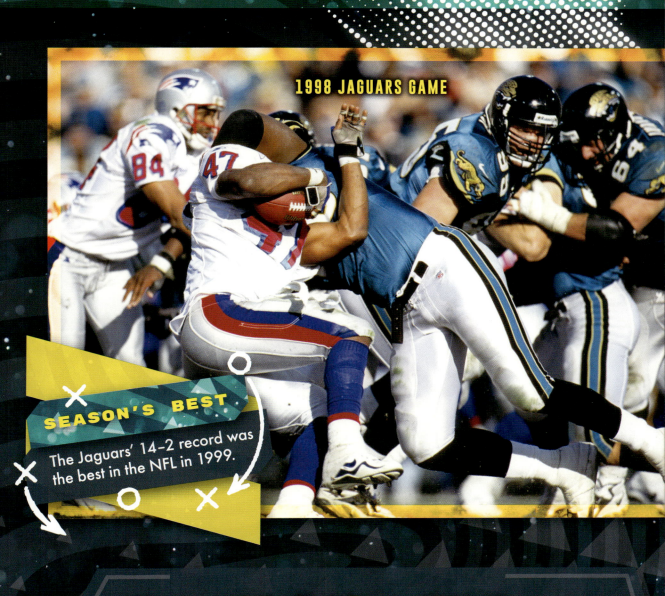

1998 JAGUARS GAME

SEASON'S BEST

The Jaguars' 14–2 record was the best in the NFL in 1999.

They won their **division** in 1998. The next year, they won 14 games and only lost 2. They won their division again!

The team struggled during the early 2000s. But by 2017, the Jaguars were known for their strong **defense**.

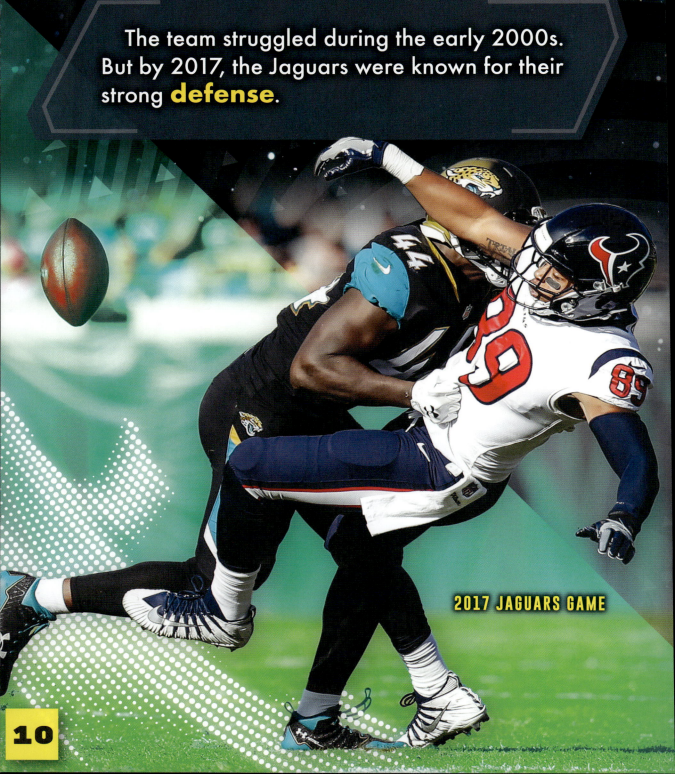

2017 JAGUARS GAME

10

They made it to the AFC **Championship** Game. But they lost to the New England Patriots.

TROPHY CASE

PLAYOFF appearances
8

AFC SOUTH championships
2

AFC CENTRAL championships
2

11

In 2021, the Jaguars added **quarterback** Trevor Lawrence to the team. The following year, Lawrence led the team to the playoffs!

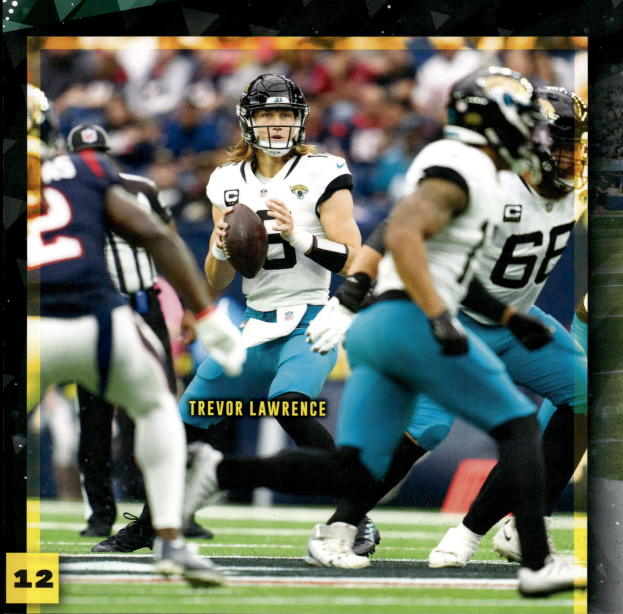

TREVOR LAWRENCE

12

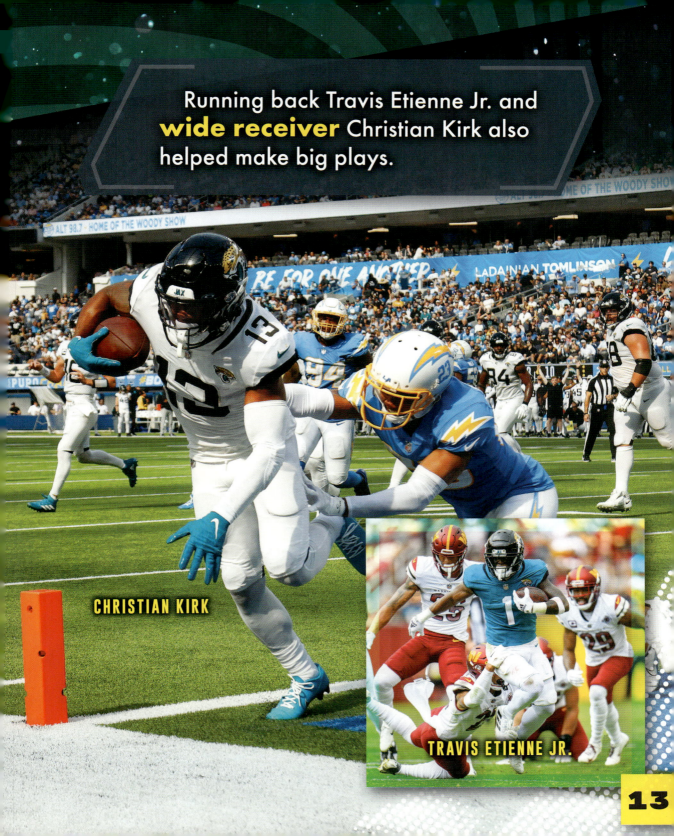

Running back Travis Etienne Jr. and **wide receiver** Christian Kirk also helped make big plays.

CHRISTIAN KIRK

TRAVIS ETIENNE JR.

THE JAGUARS TODAY

JAGUARS VS. TITANS

The Jaguars play in the AFC South. They play at TIAA Bank Field in Jacksonville, Florida.

14

Their biggest **rival** is the Tennessee Titans. The two teams often meet on the field.

◉ LOCATION ◉

TIAA BANK FIELD

Jacksonville, Florida

FLORIDA

GAME DAY!

Fans fill TIAA Bank Field on game day. They wear teal, black, and gold gear. They are loud!

The D-Line adds to the noise. They play drums to help fans cheer on their team.

D-LINE

FUN ZONE

TIAA Bank Field has a Fan Entertainment Zone. Fans can play games, throw footballs, meet former players, and more!

TIAA BANK FIELD

The Jaguars **mascot** is a big part of every game. His name is Jaxson de Ville.

Jaxson will do anything to get fans excited. He dances and rides a scooter. Jaguars fans have fun rooting for their team!

JAXSON DE VILLE

★ FAMOUS PLAYERS ★

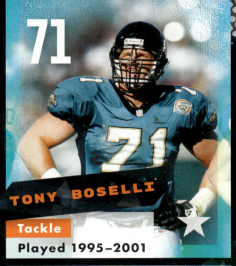

71 TONY BOSELLI
Tackle
Played 1995–2001

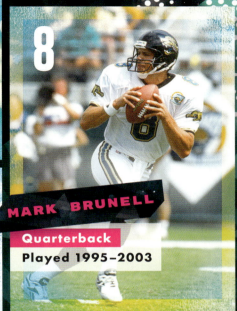

8 MARK BRUNELL
Quarterback
Played 1995–2003

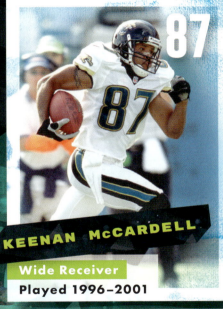

87 KEENAN McCARDELL
Wide Receiver
Played 1996–2001

28 FRED TAYLOR
Running Back
Played 1998–2008

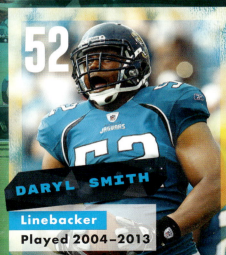

52 DARYL SMITH
Linebacker
Played 2004–2013

JACKSONVILLE JAGUARS FACTS

LOGO

JOINED THE NFL	1995

MASCOT

JAXSON DE VILLE

NICKNAME	Jags

CONFERENCE

American Football Conference (AFC)

COLORS

DIVISION | AFC South

 Houston Texans
 Indianapolis Colts
 Tennessee Titans

STADIUM

★ **TIAA BANK FIELD** ★

opened August 18, 1995

holds **67,814** people

🕒 TIMELINE

1995
The Jacksonville Jaguars play their first season

2000
The Jaguars beat the Miami Dolphins, 62–7

2022
The Jaguars make the playoffs for the eighth time

1998
The Jaguars win their division for the first time

2018
The Jaguars play in the AFC Championship Game

★ RECORDS ★

All-Time Passing Leader	All-Time Rushing Leader	Single-Season Scoring Leader	All-Time Scoring Leader

Mark Brunell
25,698 yards

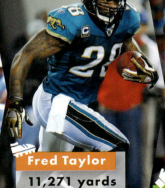
Fred Taylor
11,271 yards

Mike Hollis
134 points in 1997

Josh Scobee
1,022 points

21

GLOSSARY

championship—a contest to decide the best team or person

defense—the group of players who try to stop the opposing team from scoring

division—a group of NFL teams from the same area that often play against each other; there are eight divisions in the NFL.

mascot—an animal or symbol that represents a sports team

playoff—a game played after the regular season is over; playoff games determine which teams play in the championship game.

quarterback—a player whose main job is to throw and hand off the ball

rival—a long-standing opponent

running back—a player whose main job is to run with the ball

tackle—a player whose main job is to block for teammates

touchdown—a score that occurs when a team crosses into their opponent's end zone with the football; a touchdown is worth six points.

wide receiver—a player whose main job is to catch passes from the quarterback

TO LEARN MORE

AT THE LIBRARY

Klepeis, Alicia Z. *The Tennessee Titans*. Minneapolis, Minn.: Bellwether Media, 2024.

Meier, William. *Jacksonville Jaguars*. Minneapolis, Minn.: Abdo, 2020.

Whiting, Jim. *The Story of the Jacksonville Jaguars*. Minneapolis, Minn.: Kaleidoscope, 2020.

ON THE WEB

FACTSURFER

Factsurfer.com gives you a safe, fun way to find more information.

1. Go to www.factsurfer.com.

2. Enter "Jacksonville Jaguars" into the search box and click 🔍.

3. Select your book cover to see a list of related content.

INDEX

AFC Championship Game, 11
AFC South, 14, 20
Boselli, Tony, 6, 7
colors, 16, 20
defense, 10
division, 9, 14
D-Line, 16
Etienne, Travis, Jr., 13
famous players, 19
Fan Entertainment Zone, 17
fans, 16, 17, 18
history, 4, 5, 6, 8, 9, 10, 11, 12, 13
Jacksonville, Florida, 14, 15
Jacksonville Jaguars facts, 20–21
Kirk, Christian, 13
Lawrence, Trevor, 12
mascot, 18, 20
National Football League (NFL), 5, 6, 9, 20
playoff, 4, 5, 8, 12
positions, 4, 6, 12, 13
records, 5, 9, 21
rival, 15
Taylor, Fred, 4, 5
TIAA Bank Field, 14, 15, 16, 17, 20
timeline, 21
trophy case, 11

The images in this book are reproduced through the courtesy of: Tom DiPace/ AP Images, front cover, pp. 1, 19 (Keenan McCardell); Excel23/ Wikipedia, front cover (stadium), p. 1; Icon Sportswire/ Contributor/ Getty Images, pp. 3, 10, 16, 18-19; Al Messerschmidt Archive/ AP Images, pp. 4, 21 (1998); Joe Robbins/ AP Images, p. 5; Julian H. Gonzalez/ Stringer/ Getty Images, p. 6; George Gojkovich/ Contributor/ Getty Images, pp. 6-7; Andy Lyons/ Staff/ Getty Images, pp. 8, 21 (Mike Hollis); Allen Kee/ Contributor/ Getty Images, p. 9; Cooper Neill/ Contributor/ Getty Images, p. 12; Cal Sport Media/ Alamy, pp. 12-13, 13 (inset); Mike Carlson/ Stringer/ Getty Images, p. 14; NEFLO PHOTO, pp. 15 (TIAA Bank Field), 20 (TIAA Bank Field); NFL/ Wikipedia, pp. 15 (Jacksonville Jaguars logo), 20 (logos); Cindy Marshall/ AP Images, pp. 16-17; Focus On Sport/ Contributor/ Getty Images, pp. 19 (Tony Boselli, Mark Brunell), 21 (Mark Brunell); Sam Greenwood/ Staff/ Getty Images, pp. 19 (Fred Taylor, Daryl Smith), 21 (Fred Taylor); James Gilbert/ Contributor/ Getty Images, p. 20 (mascot); Paul Spinelli/ NFL Photos/ AP Images, p. 21 (1995); UPI/ Alamy, p. 21 (2000); Kevin C. Cox/ Staff/ Getty Images, p. 21 (2018); April Visuals, pp. 21 (2022), 23; Zuma Press, Inc./ Alamy, p. 21 (Josh Scobee).